Read & Respond

FOR KS2

Read & Respond

FOR
KS2

Author: Gillian Howell

Development Editor: Simret Brar

Editor: Victoria Lee

Assistant Editor: Frances Ridley

Series Designer/Designer: Anna Oliwa

Illustrations: Quentin Blake and Jane Bottomley

Text © Gillian Howell © 2008 Scholastic Ltd

Designed using Adobe InDesign

Published by Scholastic Ltd,
Book End, Range Road, Witney,
Oxfordshire OX29 0YD

www.scholastic.co.uk

Printed by Bell & Bain

789   34567

British Library Cataloguing-in-Publication Data
A catalogue record for this book is available from the British
Library.

ISBN 978-1407-10043-2

Acknowledgements

David Higham Associates for the use of extracts from *George's
Marvellous Medicine* by Roald Dahl © 1981, Roald Dahl (1981,
Jonathan Cape).
Random House Group for the use of illustrations by Quentin
Blake from *George's Marvellous Medicine* by Roald Dahl © 1981,
Quentin Blake, (1981 Jonathan Cape).

George's Marvellous Medicine

About the book

The appeal of Roald Dahl's books lies in children's enjoyment of risqué humour and love of justice. *George's Marvellous Medicine* follows the pattern of most of his popular stories: a lonely child who is mistreated by a cruel adult gets his own back in a startling and funny manner. It is a tale of retribution and revenge that is told with great humour and fantasy, making good use of language, alliteration and simile that could engender a love of words in young readers. It is littered with jokes and wordplay and complemented by Quentin Blake's sparse line drawings. There are 15 short chapters, which make it ideal for building reading stamina in early readers.

When George Kranky is left alone to look after his 'grizzly old grunion' of a grandma, his mother leaves him with the instructions to be good, not to get up to any mischief and to remember to give Grandma her medicine at 11 o'clock. Grandma grumbles and complains, even telling George he must stop growing, and eventually really frightens George by intimating that she knows secrets about dark places where 'dark things live and squirm and slither all over each other…'

George decides to cure Grandma of her nastiness by making her a new medicine – one that will cure her or blow her head off. He mixes up a powerful brew made from every harmful product in the house (except things from the medicine cabinet) and several animal medicines from his father's shed.

When Grandma takes a spoonful of the medicine, the effects are immediate and startling. She grows taller and taller, eventually stopping with her head sticking through the roof of the house. It has not cured her of her nastiness, but it has made her feel happier!

George's father thinks the medicine will make them rich, as it will make the animals on his farm bigger, but unfortunately George cannot remember the exact recipe. After several attempts, they create a medicine that makes things shrink. Nasty Grandma demands the medicine and drinks it all. She then begins to shrink, complaining all the time, and shrinks away into nothingness.

About the author

Roald Dahl (1916–1990) was born in Wales of Norwegian parents.

He began writing after suffering a serious plane crash, first writing for adults then, later, telling and writing stories for his own children. He wrote in a shed at the bottom of the garden, full of dust and spiders, that no one else was ever allowed to enter. For inspiration, he drew on his own childhood experiences at boarding school for many of his plots and characters, skilfully mixing real-life situations with pure fantasy. He went on to write 21 successful children's books, several of which have been made into films and plays.

Facts and figures

Roald Dahl's work has been translated into 34 languages. In 1983 his book *The Witches* won the Whitbread Award. In 1989 he won the Children's Book Award for *Matilda*.

Guided reading

Introducing the book

Begin by asking the children if they know the name Roald Dahl. They may already be familiar with some of his other stories on film or through reading. Ask them to describe some of the characters they remember and compare any similarities from different books, for example: adults are often horrible and the main character is mistreated in some way.

Focus attention on the cover illustration. Point out the face at the top of the cover. Ask them who they think this might be. Read the title and ask the children to say who the boy is and what they think he is doing. Turn to the back cover and read the blurb. Ask the children to suggest what effect George's own special brew will have on Grandma.

If any of the group have already read or listened to *George's Marvellous Medicine*, explain that reading it again in the group will help them explore the story in greater detail.

'Grandma' and 'The Marvellous Plan'

In the first two chapters, Grandma's nastiness is established, and the reader's sympathies for George's predicament are developed. George begins to make plans for getting even with Grandma and readers believe she deserves it.

Read the opening paragraph with the group and ask them what they think George will do in the story. (George will get up to mischief.) Ask them if they think this is an effective way to begin a story. Does it make them want to find out what the mischief will be?

Ask the children to read to the end of 'The Marvellous Plan' and then describe what Grandma is like. Tell them to find the descriptive words and phrases in the text. (For example: 'wicked little eye'; 'grizzly old grunion'; 'selfish, grumpy old woman'; 'pale brown teeth'; 'small puckered-up mouth like a dog's bottom'.) Point out the use of alliteration in 'grizzly old grunion' and ask them to find any other examples. (For

instance, 'grousing, grouching, grumbling, griping'.)

Discuss the things that Grandma says to George. Ask the children whether they think Grandma's instructions to George about what he should eat are silly, sensible or frightening. Look at pages 9 to 11. Ask them where and how the tone and atmosphere changes. How does George feel about Grandma and what frightens him most, her words or her appearance?

Turn to page 12 and encourage the children to describe the ideas George has before he makes the medicine. Look at the text and point out the use of italics. Ask what effect the italics have on the way the sentences are read. Invite the children to read them aloud with expressive voices. Talk about how the chapter ends. Does it heighten their wish to find out what happens next?

'George Begins to Make the Medicine', 'Animal Pills' and 'The Cook-up'

Ask the children to read these chapters. George finds ingredients for his medicine from all over the house and in his father's shed. Many of the ingredients he chooses have a particular purpose, for example, 'GOLDEN GLOSS HAIR SHAMPOO' should 'wash her tummy nice and clean'. Roald Dahl includes lots of alliterative phrases and humour to describe the ingredients, for example, 'FOR HORSES WITH HOARSE THROATS'.

Turn to page 17 and ask the children what 'rule' George makes up for creating the medicine. Ask them if they think this is a good idea, and why or why not. Turn to pages 18 and 19. Ask why he does not use anything from the medicine cabinet. What does this tell us about George? (He is good and obeys his parents. He does not actually want to kill Grandma with the medicine.)

Ask the children to scan pages 19 to 25 to find the names of the ingredients in the order that he uses them and, where appropriate, say what effect he thinks they will have on Grandma. Invite them to choose which one they find the most humorous and say why.

Turn to 'Animal Pills' and read the opening paragraphs. Ask the children if they think George should use the animal medicines. Point out the sentence: 'He knew his father wouldn't be there.' What does this sentence tell them about the rights or wrongs of George's decision?

Ask them what the similarities are between this chapter and the previous chapter. (It describes each ingredient with humour and builds up anticipation about the effect of the medicine.) How does George refer to Grandma with each medicine? (For example, medicine for chickens – 'the old bird'.)

Look at 'The Cook-up'. Encourage the children to find the words in the text that describe the medicine as it is cooking. Ask them to identify the adjectives used and the alliterative phrases. Read the sentence beginning: 'It was a brutal and bewitching smell…' How does this description make the children feel? Does it make them excited about the medicine? Read the poem together. Talk about the use of alliteration, internal rhyme and find the onomatopoeic words. ('Fizzle swizzle'; 'sloshing, swashing, sploshing'; 'hissing, squishing, spissing'). Which words are invented words?

'Brown Paint' and 'Grandma Gets the Medicine'

Let the children read these chapters. The effects of George's medicine are revealed, as Grandma grows so tall she bursts through the upper floors of the house and George is worried about what his parents will say.

Ask the children to turn to 'Brown Paint'. Can the children explain why Grandma would be suspicious if the medicine is not brown? Ask them to read the words Grandma says at the foot of page 35 and the top of page 36. Why has the author used exclamation marks here? What effect does this have on the way the words are read? Point out that Grandma again tells George he is growing too fast. Why does Dahl add this at

this point in the story? (It is ironic that Grandma grows extremely fast after she has taken the medicine.) Ask the children to read the end of the chapter aloud, from the line, 'Medicine time, Grandma!' Why do they think the author ends the chapter here? (To create suspense.)

Turn to 'Grandma Gets the Medicine' and look at page 39. Read together George's remembrance of how he created the medicine. Can the children think of anything he has forgotten? Point out the punctuation at the foot of the page. Why has the author used ellipses between each phrase? What effect does this have on the way the words are read? (Dramatic pauses.)

Encourage the children to describe what happens to Grandma when she takes the medicine, in the order it happens. Look together at the second paragraph on page 42. Talk about the language Grandma uses to describe how she feels. Let the children suggest what 'jacky-jumpers' and 'squigglers' might feel like. Turn to page 47 and ask them how Grandma feels now. Encourage the children to read the text on page 49 using expressive voices.

'The Brown Hen' and 'The Pig, the Bullocks, the Sheep, the Pony and the Nanny-goat'

The effect of the medicine is revealed and George's father, Mr Kranky, realises that the medicine will make his farm animals bigger, making him more money. Let the children read the chapters.

Ask the group to describe what happens. Why does George give the hen a spoonful of medicine? (To prove to Grandma that he made it.) How does Grandma react to the growing hen? (She boasts that she is the tallest and wants to be the centre of attention.) Encourage the children to find another example of Grandma demanding attention in 'The Pig, the Bullocks, the Sheep, the Pony and the Nanny-goat'. Invite the children to describe how George's father reacts to Grandma. Is he surprised to see her sticking out of the roof? How does he react to the giant hen?

Guided reading

'A Crane for Grandma' and 'Mr Kranky's Great Idea'

Grandma's selfish personality is emphasised as she loses centre stage. Mr Kranky's personality is also brought out, as he gets carried away with plans to make money through George's medicine, and George attempts to recreate the ingredients.

Let the children read the two chapters. Ask them to describe how Grandma reacts when she is released from the house by the crane. Can they find any further alliterative phrases? (For example, 'frisky as a ferret'; 'miserable midgets'.)

Ask them what Mr Kranky's motive is for wanting to produce more of George's medicine: to be able to produce food for the world, or to make himself rich? Encourage the children to make a note of the ingredients that George remembers. Do they think he has left anything out?

The chapter ends with Mr Kranky asking George to tell him exactly how he mixed all the ingredients togehter. Ask the children us they think George will be able to remember exactly what he did, and why or why not. Before they read the next chapter, ask the group to try to remember exactly what George did.

'Marvellous Medicine Number Two' to the end

In the final chapters, Grandma receives a cruel and final justice for her nastiness. Before the children begin reading, ask them to predict whether George will remember the ingredients this time and what effects the medicine might have.

Encourage the children to focus on Mrs Kranky. Ask them to think of any words to describe her character (for example, calm, sensible, realistic) and to find evidence in the text to support their suggestions.

Ask them what Grandma thinks Medicine Number Four is. Ask why Mr Kranky 'smiled sweetly' when he tells Grandma to drink it. Turn to page 102. Why has the author used ellipses here? How do the illustrations help the reader to understand what is happening to Grandma?

Look at the last paragraph of the story and ask the children if they think this is a good way to end *George's Marvellous Medicine* and why.

Shared reading

Extract 1

● Ask the children who already knows the story. Recap what has happened in the opening chapter and explain that this extract comes at the beginning of 'The Marvellous Plan', just after Grandma has really frightened George. Can the children empathise with George?

● Read the first paragraph and encourage the children to read aloud with you, using expressive voices to emphasise the italic words.

● Read from 'I'm not going to be frightened by her.. ' up to '...exploding shocker for Grandma?' together. Do the children think George wants to hurt Grandma? Ask them to find words in the text to support their answer. What does George really want to do to Grandma?

● Mask the adjectives in the phrase 'whopping terrific exploding shocker'. Reveal the adjectives one by one, re-reading the phrase each time. What effect do these adjectives have? Ask them to suggest why the author chose to use them.

● Read George's three ideas of what he would like to do to Grandma. Discuss his ideas and how Grandma might react to each of them. Were they good ideas?

● Speculate what George might be thinking when he sees the bottle.

Extract 2

● This extract is from 'Animal Pills'. George has obeyed the rule about not touching the medicine cabinet but, realising it does not apply to the animals' medicines, he adds these pills and potions to the mixture. What do the children notice about the way the words have been written?

● Ask the children why the author uses upper-case letters to describe the medicines. Does it have an effect on the way they read it? What does the author tell you about the appearance of the medicines? (Colour and texture.)

● Read each description and discuss which of the animal illnesses are genuine and which are invented. Point out the play on words 'horse' and 'hoarse' and the allusion to 'The House that Jack Built' ('crumpled horns'). What effect does the author intend these descriptions to have?

● How does George relate each of the medicines to Grandma? Highlight the words in the text.

● Ask pairs to choose which description and George's comment they think is the most amusing and to say why. Invite them to read their choice aloud.

Extract 3

● This extract, from the final chapter 'Goodbye Grandma', comes just after Mr Kranky and George test their fourth attempt at the medicine.

● The passage contains a great deal of direct speech. Point out how a change of speaker always begins on a new line. Highlight the punctuation used in writing dialogue.

● Tell the children to find the exclamation marks in the first paragraph. Encourage them to read the sentences out loud and say what effect the punctuation has on how they say the words.

● Ask them how Mr Kranky's response to Grandma differs from that of George and his mother.

● Arrange the children into groups of four. Let them take the role of one character each and read the dialogue aloud using expressive voices.

● Point out the ellipsis that ends Mrs Kranky's words. Ask the chidlren to suggest why Mrs Kranky was unable to finish what she was saying and what is missing.

● Ask them to predict what Grandma, George or Mrs or Mr Kranky will do immediately after this point.

Extract 1

The Marvellous Plan

George sat himself down at the table in the kitchen. He was shaking a little. Oh, how he hated Grandma! He really *hated* that horrid old witchy woman. And all of a sudden he had a tremendous urge to *do something* about her. Something *whopping*. Something *absolutely terrific*. A *real shocker*. A sort of explosion. He wanted to blow away the witchy smell that hung about her in the next room. He may have been only eight years old but he was a brave little boy. He was ready to take this old woman on.

'I'm not going to be frightened by *her*,' he said softly to himself. But he *was* frightened. And that's why he wanted suddenly to explode her away.

Well … not quite away. But he did want to shake the old woman up a bit.

Very well, then. What should it be, this whopping terrific exploding shocker for Grandma?

He would have liked to put a firework banger under her chair but he didn't have one.

He would have liked to put a long green snake down the back of her dress but he didn't have a long green snake.

He would have liked to put six big black rats in the room with her and lock the door but he didn't have six big black rats.

As George sat there pondering this interesting problem, his eye fell upon the bottle of Grandma's brown medicine standing on the sideboard.

Illustration © Quentin Blake

Extract 2

Animal Pills

The first bottle he took down contained an orange-coloured powder. The label said, FOR CHICKENS WITH FOUL PEST, HEN GRIPE, SORE BEAKS, GAMMY LEGS, COCKERELITIS, EGG TROUBLE, BROODINESS OR LOSS OF FEATHERS. MIX ONE SPOONFUL ONLY WITH EACH BUCKET OF FEED.

'Well,' George said aloud to himself as he tipped in the whole bottleful, 'the old bird won't be losing any feathers after she's had a dose of this.'

The next bottle he took down had about five hundred gigantic purple pills in it. FOR HORSES WITH HOARSE THROATS, it said on the label. THE HOARSE-THROATED HORSE SHOULD SUCK ONE PILL TWICE A DAY.

'Grandma may not have a hoarse throat,' George said, 'but she's certainly got a sharp tongue. Maybe they'll cure that instead.' Into the saucepan went the five hundred gigantic purple pills.

Then there was a bottle of thick yellowish liquid. FOR COWS, BULLS AND BULLOCKS, the label said. WILL CURE COW POX, COW MANGE, CRUMPLED HORNS, BAD BREATH IN BULLS, EARACHE, TOOTHACHE, HEADACHE, HOOFACHE, TAILACHE AND SORE UDDERS.

'That grumpy old cow in the living-room has every one of those rotten illnesses,' George said. 'She'll need it all.' With a slop and a gurgle, the yellow liquid splashed into the now nearly full saucepan.

Illustration © Quentin Blake

Extract 3

Goodbye Grandma

Just then, the old woman spotted the cup in George's hand. She bent down and peered into it. She saw that it was full of brown liquid. It looked very much like tea. 'Ho-ho!' she cried. 'Ha-ha! So that's your little game, is it! You look after yourself all right, don't you! You make quite sure *you've* got a nice cup of morning tea! But you didn't think to bring one to your poor old Grandma! I always knew you were a selfish pig!'

'No, Grandma,' George said. 'This isn't…'

'Don't lie to me, boy!' the enormous old hag shouted. 'Pass it up here this minute!'

'No!' cried Mrs Kranky. 'No, Mother, don't! That's not for you!'

'Now *you're* against me, too!' shouted Grandma. 'My own daughter trying to stop me having my breakfast! Trying to starve me out!'

Mr Kranky looked up at the horrid old woman and he smiled sweetly. 'Of course it's for you, Grandma,' he said. 'You take it and drink it while it's nice and hot.'

'Don't think I won't,' Grandma said, bending down from her great height and reaching out a huge horny hand for the cup. 'Hand it over, George.'

'No, no, Grandma!' George cried out, pulling the cup away. 'You mustn't! You're not to have it!'

'Give it to me, boy!' yelled Grandma.

'Don't!' cried Mrs Kranky. 'That's George's Marvellous…'

Illustration © Quentin Blake

READ & RESPOND: Activities based on *George's Marvellous Medicine*

Plot, character and setting

Grandma

> **Objective:** To empathise with characters.
> **What you need:** Copies of *George's Marvellous Medicine*.
> **Cross-curricular links:** PSHE; Citizenship.

What to do
● Invite the children to read 'Grandma' and then, in pairs, find and make a note of all the words and phrases that describe Grandma's appearance. Go through their lists as a class and discuss the author's choice of adjectives. Why does Roald Dahl say, for example, 'wicked little eye' and 'thin icy smile'? How do these descriptions make them *feel* about Grandma?
● Then ask the pairs to note the words and phrases that describe her personality. Go through their lists and identify alliteration and invented vocabulary, for example, 'grizzly old grunion'.
● Now focus on the things Grandma says to George, beginning with: 'You know what's the matter with you?' Can the children say *why* they think Grandma says these things? Ask them to find any words and phrases that tell readers *how* she says them.
● Invite them to add words of their own to the list describing her personality, based on how they think her words make George feel.
● Ask the pairs to share their ideas with the class. Compare some of the words the children chose themselves to describe Grandma's personality. Revisit the list of words and phrases that describe Grandma's appearance. How does her appearance reflect her personality? Invite the children to suggest other stories where a character's appearance reflects their personality.

> **Differentiation**
> **For older/more confident learners:** Ask the children to write a character description of Grandma.
> **For younger/less confident learners:** Let the children draw Grandma and label the drawing.

George

> **Objective:** To empathise with characters.
> **What you need:** Copies of *George's Marvellous Medicine*, enlarged copies of photocopiable page 15.

What to do
● Explain that authors sometimes give explicit information about the characters in a story and sometimes give clues about their motives and thoughts. This makes readers feel more involved in the story because they can think for themselves and interpret the author's words. Explain that this is 'inference' or 'reading between the lines'.
● Read the opening paragraph aloud to the children. Ask them to say what this tells them about George's mother, for example, does the act of leaving him at home mean she actually trusts him not to get up to mischief? What do her words tell them about George? Do they imply that he usually does get up to mischief?
● Discuss George's character and personality. Ask them what the author tells them explicitly and what they infer from George's actions. What do they think are George's motives for making the medicine?
● Ask children to work in pairs and provide each pair with a copy of Photocopiable page 15. Invite them to discuss their ideas about George's motives. Then they should scan the text to find relevant information for their answers.

> **Differentiation**
> **For older/more confident learners:** Mask all the words on the photocopiable page apart from the first one on each line. Invite the children to write their own poems modelled on the text.
> **For younger/less confident learners:** Tell the children not to worry about the rhyme but to concentrate on using imaginative language.

Plot, character and setting

Rooms

> **Objective:** To experiment with the order of sections.
> **What you need:** Copies of *George's Marvellous Medicine*, photocopiable page 16, scissors.
> **Cross-curricular links:** PSHE.

What to do
● Ask the children to do this activity after they have finished 'Brown Paint'.
● Challenge the children to remember all the ingredients George uses to make his medicine, without referring to the text. Draw up a list.
● Now encourage them to remember the different places George went to find the ingredients. Can they remember them in the correct sequence?
● Using the class list as a reference, ask them to return to the text and scan the pages to find any missing ingredients or places. Add these to the list, matching the places to the things George found. Let the children read the list one last time, and then erase it.
● Ask the children to work in pairs to complete photocopiable page 16. Tell them to add the ingredients they remember to the correct column of the sheet. They should keep checking with their partner so they include as many as possible. Then ask the children to cut out each column and sequence them in the order they occurred in the story.
● Invite the children to describe their results orally, beginning: *First George went…* Encourage them to use connectives to sequence the rows, for example: Next, After that, Finally.

> **Differentiation**
> **For older/more confident learners:** Encourage the children to add extra detail about colour to each item on their list.
> **For younger/less confident learners:** Ask the children to draw the ingredients instead of writing them.

The view

> **Objective:** To understand points of view.
> **What you need:** Copies of *George's Marvellous Medicine*, photocopiable page 17.

What to do
● Ask the children to read 'Grandma Gets the Medicine' and 'The Brown Hen'. To ensure the children understand what has happened, ask them to describe to a partner the sequence of events in these two chapters.
● Discuss the point of view of the story: it is told from George's point of view. Ask the children to think of questions they would like to ask Grandma about what happened from *her* point of view, using What, When, Where, and Why.
● Choose children to sit in the hot seat as Grandma. Can they answer questions in role?
● Then ask the children to find examples in the text that describe how Grandma feels, for example: she feels grumpy when George comes in, and feels happy and proud once she has stopped growing.
● Encourage them to put themselves into Grandma's place and to imagine what she might be thinking on pages 41, 46 and 47, 50 and 51, and page 58.
● Hand out photocopiable page 17. Ask the children to imagine they are Grandma looking out from the roof, and write what they are seeing, saying, thinking and feeling.

> **Differentiation**
> **For older/more confident learners:** Ask the children to use their ideas on the photocopiable page to write a first-person description of Grandma.
> **For younger/less confident learners:** Blank out two of the shapes from the photocopiable page, for example, leaving only the speech bubble and the thought bubble.

Plot, character and setting

Setting

> **Objective:** To use settings to engage readers' interest.
> **What you need:** Copies of *George's Marvellous Medicine*, large sheets of paper and pens or pencils.
> **Cross-curricular links:** Geography.

What to do

● Run this activity when the children have finished reading 'The Pig, the Bullocks, the Sheep, the Pony and the Nanny-goat'.
● Ask the children to describe where the story takes place. (In the house and farmyard.) Encourage them to add as many details as they can, for example: rooms inside the house; 'a fine roof of pale red tiles and tall chimneys'; a garage and a shed in the farmyard; the animals in the farmyard setting. Encourage them to think carefully about where the animals would be found in the setting, and to find any evidence in the story, for example, hens in the yard and pigs in the pigsty.
● Explain to the children that you want them to create a picture-plan of the setting that shows the buildings and farm animals. Tell them to draw the buildings on to their plans, and to add labels to describe what they are, for example, *stable*. They can add captions to describe some of the events, for example, *This is where George found the animal medicines*. Ask them to use their imaginations to arrange the farm animals and their locations around the farm. Compare the completed picture plans.

> **Differentiation**
> **For older/more confident learners:** Ask the children to write a character description of Grandma.
> **For younger/less confident learners:** Let the children draw Grandma and label the drawing.

Mr Killy Kranky

> **Objective:** To deduce characters' reasons for behaviour from their actions.
> **What you need:** Copies of *George's Marvellous Medicine*.

What to do

● Begin this activity before the children read 'Mr Kranky's Great Idea'.
● Ask the children, in pairs, to discuss the character of Mr Kranky. How does Mr Kranky interact with the other characters, George, Grandma and Mrs Kranky? Can they suggest what sort of person he is, finding evidence in the story up to 'Mr Kranky's Great Idea'? (For example, in 'The Pig, the Bullocks, the Sheep, the Pony and the Nanny-goat', he is 'a kind father'.)
● Draw up a list of adjectives and phrases from the children's ideas.
● Tell the class to read 'Mr Kranky's Great Idea' and 'Marvellous Medicine Number Two', and focus again on what Mr Kranky says and does.
Are there any new words and phrases to add to the list?
● Ask the children to write a character sketch of Mr Kranky. Model how to begin, for example: *Although Mr Kranky is a kind father to George, he is not easy to live with.* Encourage the children to suggest the next sentence.
● Give the children two headings to help them organise content: *Mr Kranky and Grandma* and *Mr Kranky and the medicine*. Ask the children to write two paragraphs describing Mr Kranky.
● Invite some children to read their paragraph aloud. Discuss similarities and differences.

> **Differentiation**
> **For older/more confident learners:** Ask the children to write more than two paragraphs without using the headings.
> **For younger/less confident learners:** Tell the children to write one paragraph about Mr Kranky.

Plot, character and setting

Cause and effect

> **Objective:** To make notes on and use evidence from across a text to explain events.
> **What you need:** Copies of *George's Marvellous Medicine*, photocopiable page 18, scissors and glue.

What to do

● Look together at the 'Contents' page and discuss the sequence of events. Encourage the children to think about how one event is connected to the next, for example: Grandma's nastiness to George leads to his plan for giving her a shock, so he begins to make the medicine. Explain that recognising cause and effect helps them to understand why characters behave in certain ways and how their actions affect the plot. Ask them to use the chapter headings to find examples of cause and effect.

● Allow five to ten minutes for a paired activity.

One child finds an event in the book and describes it by saying, *What happened when….* The other child answers, working from memory. Then they swap roles.

● Hand out photocopiable page 18. Ask the children to work individually to complete the sentences, cut out the rows and rearrange them in the correct sequence of events. Tell them to stick the rows onto paper.

● Select children to read their completed sentences.

> **Differentiation**
> **For older/more confident learners:** Ask the children to add two or three more examples of cause and effect to the sequence.
> **For younger/less confident learners:** Before copying the photocopiable page, blank out 'so...' Ask the children to sequence the sentences.

Recipe

> **Objective:** To compare different types of narrative and information texts.
> **What you need:** Copies of *George's Marvellous Medicine*.

What to do

● Ask the children to list all the things George uses to make Medicine Number One. Invite them to scan from 'George Begins to Make the Medicine' to the end of 'Brown Paint' to create a list of ingredients for a recipe:

Shampoo	Toothpaste	Shaving soap
Face cream	Nail varnish	Hair remover
Dandruff cure	False-teeth cleaner	Deodorant
Paraffin	Hairspray	Perfume
Face Powder	2 Lipsticks	Washing powder
Floor polish	Flea powder	Canary seed
Shoe polish	Gin	Curry powder
Mustard powder	Chilli sauce	Peppercorns
Horseradish sauce	Chicken medicine	Horse pills
Cow medicine	Sheepdip	Pig pills
Engine oil	Anti-freeze	Grease
Brown gloss paint		

● Explain that the children are going to write a set of instructions in groups, each group taking a different set of ingredients. Say that instructions use command verbs (Mix, Stir and so on), and might also contain time-related connectives (First, Next, Finally). Model how to begin.

● Divide the ingredients, so that each group has a similar number, and ask the groups to complete a set of instructions.

● Arrange each group's instructions into the order of the story as a display.

> **Differentiation**
> **For older/more confident learners:** Let the children work in smaller groups.
> **For younger/less confident learners:** Provide the children with different command verbs and support them in constructing their sentences.

George

Think about these questions.	Write your answers in this column.
Why did George dive for the door?	
Why did George change from wanting to explode Grandma away to wanting to shake her up a bit?	
Why did George choose to make a new medicine?	
Why did George add GOLDEN GLOSS HAIR SHAMPOO?	
Why did George add a whole bottle of gin?	
Why did George add a handful of grease?	
Why did George ask if Grandma was going to gulp down the medicine or sip it?	
Why did George get a jugful of water?	
What did George feel while Grandma was getting taller and taller?	
Why did George refuse to give Grandma Marvellous Medicine number 4?	
Why did George feel quite trembly?	

Rooms

- List the things George found for his medicine in each column under the correct place.

Kitchen	Shoe-cleaning box	Garage	Bathroom	On his way back to the kitchen	Bedroom	Laundry-room	Shed

The view

● Imagine you are Grandma looking out from the roof. Write what you can see, what you are thinking, what you might say and how you feel.

Illustration © Quentin Blake

Cause and effect

● Finish each sentence, then cut them out and arrange the events of the story in the correct sequence.

George's medicine is blue, so…

Medicine Number Two makes a chicken have long legs, so…

Grandma thinks George is holding a cup of tea, so…

Grandma frightens George, so…

Medicine Number Three gives a chicken a long neck, so…

Grandma thinks George is lying about making his medicine, so…

A teaspoon of Medicine Number Four makes things shrink, so…

Mr Kranky wants to be rich, so…

Talk about it

Grandma's true nature

Objective: To present a spoken argument… defending views with evidence and making use of persuasive language.
What you need: Photocopiable page 22, scissors.
Cross-curricular links: PSHE.

What to do
● Remind the children about the opening chapter 'Grandma', when readers are introduced to Grandma's character. How might Grandma feel, having to sit on her own all day?
● Write the following statement on the board: *Grandma is really a kind old lady who just likes teasing George!*
● Discuss the statement with the children and invite them to give their opinion of Grandma, supporting their views with examples from the chapter.
● Working in pairs, tell the children to put themselves into Grandma's place. Hand out photocopiable page 22 and ask the children to decide which comments are true and which are not. Encourage them to add their own ideas of what Grandma might feel and think about George. Explain that they can add 'nice' or 'nasty' comments.
● Ask the pairs to think about how they could portray Grandma as a kind old lady who is badly treated by George. Invite some of the pairs to give a brief talk to persuade the class that Grandma is really a kind old lady.
● Ask the class to hold a vote on which pair's talk was the most convincing.

Differentiation
For older/more able children: Let the children work individually on the brief talk.
For younger/less able children: Invite the children to cut out the speech bubbles and group them into two piles: true and false.

Hot seat

Objective: To create roles showing how behaviour can be interpreted from different viewpoints.
What you need: Copies of *George's Marvellous Medicine*.
Cross-curricular links: PSHE.

What to do
● This activity will follow on perfectly from the previous discussion about Grandma's true nature.
● Encourage the children to recall the events that happen to Grandma in the story. If necessary, children can refer to the text. Arrange the children into small groups of three or four. Give each group a different question word: How, Who, Where, Which, Why, What, When. Ask them each to think of a different question to ask Grandma, using the group's word to begin their own individual question. Ensure the children collaborate in their groups and compare each other's questions, so that they all have a different one to ask but beginning with the same question word, for example: *When you took the medicine…?, When did you begin to grow?* and so on.
● Ask for volunteers or select children to sit in the hot seat in the role of Grandma. Remind them about the discussion of Grandma's true nature and invite some volunteers to act as 'nice' Grandma and others to act as 'nasty' Grandma. Encourage the rest of the children to ask Grandma a question, taking one question from one group at a time, until all their questions have been asked.
● Discuss the role play. Has it given them more insight into why Grandma was nasty to George?

Differentiation
For older/more able children: Encourage them to 'perform' the role of Grandma using expressive voices and actions.
For younger/less able children: Ask the group to collaborate to choose one question only.

Talk about it

Medicine mind map

> **Objective:** To experiment with the order of sections.
> **What you need:** Copies of *George's Marvellous Medicine*, photocopiable page 23, scissors.
> **Cross-curricular links:** PSHE.

What to do

● Display the enlarged photocopiable page. Tell the class that this is an organiser that can be useful for creating a mind map of events. Briefly model how to fill in one or two of George's ingredients in the section 'Bedroom'. Demonstrate how to add other branches when needed.

● Distribute enlarged copies of photocopiable page 23. Explain that you are going to read 'George Begins to Make the Medicine' and 'Animal Pills' and, as the children listen, they should make notes of what ingredients George uses and where he finds them. Remind the children to use brief language, key words and abbreviations. Say that the audience for their notes will be a different child in the class, so they need to be legible and easily understood.

● When you have finished, ask the children to swap their mind maps with a partner and compare notes and organisation. Tell them to discuss together whether each partner's notes make sense and are easily understood.

● Let the children add any other details onto their mind map and to illustrate them.

● Invite the children to suggest when creating a mind map could help them.

> **Differentiation**
> **For older/more confident learners:** Ask the children to make mind maps without using the photocopiable page.
> **For younger/less confident learners:** Read only one of the two chapters. Ask the children to note only the ingredients and where they are found.

Making a medicine

> **Objective:** To use the techniques of dialogic talk to explore ideas, topics or issues.
> **What you need:** Copies of *George's Marvellous Medicine*, an object for each group to show whose turn it is to speak (for example, a soft toy or similar).
> **Cross-curricular links:** PSHE.

What to do

● Talk together about all the different things George puts into his marvellous medicine. Let the children refer back to the book if they cannot remember, or prompt them as necessary. Discuss with the children which of the ingredients are harmless and which are not.

● To help the chidlren clarify their thinking about each of the ingredients, write two headings 'Dangerous' and 'Harmless'. List the ingredients under the appropriate heading.

● Ask the class to think about whether George was clever to make the medicine, or if it was a dangerous thing to do.

● Arrange the children into groups and give each group an object to hold. Ask the children to take turns to speak, giving an opinion with a reason to support their idea. Ensure each child has an uninterrupted turn by using the object to pass from child to child. While a child is holding the prop, only they are allowed to speak. Encourage the children to each come up with a different reason.

● Invite the children to suggest which opinions and reasons given were the most logical or sensible.

> **Differentiation**
> For older/more **confident learners:** Invite one child from each group to summarise their group's discussion for the class. Do the children in each group mainly agree or disagree with each other?
> For younger/less **confident learners:** Monitor the discussion to ensure the children think of valid reasons to support their ideas.

Talk about it

Giant animals

Objective: To use some drama strategies to explore stories or issues.
What you need: Photocopiable page 24, card or thick paper, pencils and crayons or paint, straws or round-ended sticks, glue or Blu-Tack.
Cross-curricular links: Art and design; Drama.

What to do

● Arrange the children into groups of five. Give each group a copy of Photocopiable page 24 and an enlarged copy of Photocopiable page 24. Ask them to cut out and colour a small and a large version of a hen, pig, sheep, horse and nanny-goat. Instruct them to cut around each shape and glue them onto the straws or sticks to make stick puppets.`

● Explain that each group is going to use the puppets to create a short scene from the story when George and Mr Killy Kranky go around the farm giving the medicine to the animals. Ask the groups to share the roles of George, his father and each animal between themselves and practise the scene. Encourage them to make up dialogue and sound effects for their enactment.

● When they have had sufficient time to work out their scenes, ask the groups to put on a performance for the rest of the class.

● When each group has performed their scenes, discuss what the role-plays had in common with each other and how they were different. Ask the children which ones worked best and why.

Differentiation
For older/more **confident learners:** Ask the children to add in one or two other characters from the story.`
For younger/less **confident learners:** Provide the children with a single sentence for George and one for his father, for example: Mr Kranky: *Let's give some to the…* George: *Open wide!* Encourage them to add animal sounds.

A magic medicine it shall be!

Objective: To understand different ways to take the lead and support others in groups.
What you need: Copies of *George's Marvellous Medicine*
Cross-curricular links: Drama.

What to do

● Arrange the children into groups. Ask the groups to read the poem on pages 15 to 16 aloud together in chorus a few times until they become quite familiar with it.

● Ask for a volunteer to lead each group, or select a child for the task. Explain that the leader of the group should assign lines to each group member and then they should perform the poem again, each member reading their own lines in the correct order.

● Invite them then to swap leaders. Tell the new leaders that they should re-assign the lines and repeat the reading. Let the children continue swapping leaders, until each group member has had a turn at leading the group.

● Ask the children to discuss their different performances, and to choose together which worked best. Encourage the children to be positive about each other's performances.

● Let each group in turn perform their preferred version of the poem to the rest of the class.

● Turn to page 34. Ask the children to read the poem silently to themselves and to think how it could be performed. Should lines be shared between groups or read chorally? Read by individuals or groups? Ask for suggestions and as a class choose how to perform the poem.

Differentiation
For older/more confident learners: Let the children work in smaller groups and/or perform more lines.
For younger/less confident learners: Provide extra support, or organise groups by mixed ability, so that more able children can support less able ones.

Talk about it

Grandma's true nature

● Read these comments that Grandma might make from her point of view.

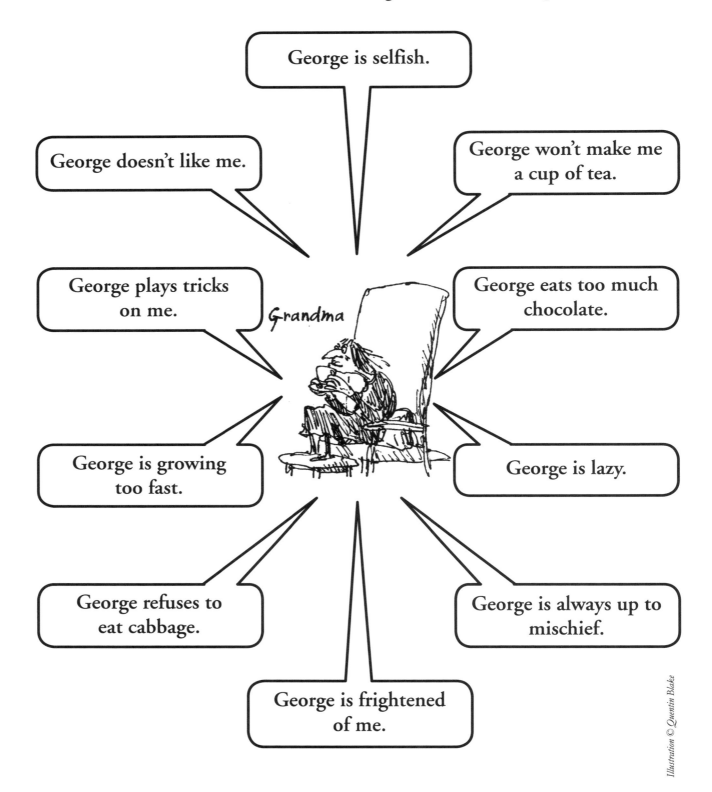

George is selfish.

George doesn't like me.

George won't make me a cup of tea.

George plays tricks on me.

Grandma

George eats too much chocolate.

George is growing too fast.

George is lazy.

George refuses to eat cabbage.

George is always up to mischief.

George is frightened of me.

Illustration © Quentin Blake

READ & RESPOND: Activities based on George's Marvellous Medicine

Medicine mind map

● Write key words and phrases to record George's ingredients.

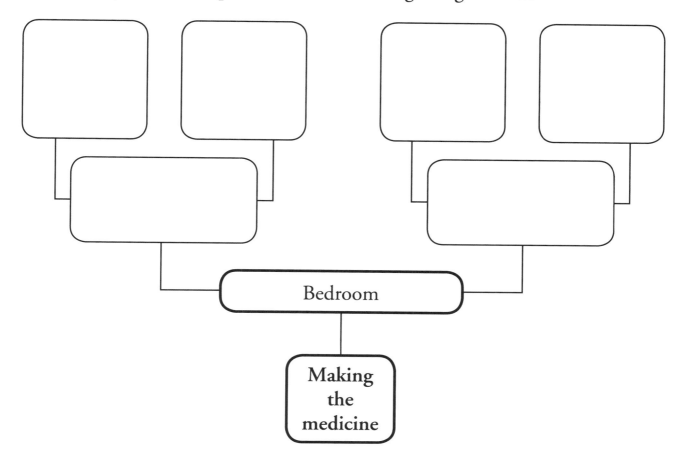

Bedroom

Making the medicine

Giant animals

● Cut around the outline of each animal to make large and small stick puppets.

Illustration © Jane Bottomley

Get writing

George's new sister

> **Objective:** To use characterisation to engage readers' interest.
> **What you need:** Copies of *George's Marvellous Medicine*, small whiteboards, photocopiable page 28.
> **Cross-curricular links:** PSHE.

What to do

● After the children have finished the book, ask them to revisit the first page of 'Grandma', beginning: 'George was bored to tears.' How might George's life be different, or similar, if he had a sister? Say that George, his parents and Grandma still have the same characteristics. Would the plot be enhanced by an elder, responsible sister or a younger, impressionable sister?

● Put the children in pairs to discuss how an elder or younger sister might respond to George's marvellous plan. Take feedback, and ask the children to decide her age together. (Remind them that George is eight.)

● Encourage the children to quickly write three adjectives to describe George's sister on their whiteboards. Compare their ideas and write good ones on the board.

● Ask them to write a sentence about how the sister feels about Grandma. Add good ideas to the board. Do the same for her feelings to George.

● Hand out photocopiable page 28. Explain that this is to help them plan a character sketch for the sister. Ask the children to write brief notes on the organiser.

● Ask some of the children to sit in the hot seat in the character of the sister and encourage the others to ask them questions.

> **Differentiation**
> **For older/more able children:** Ask the children to write a sketch for the sister, using their notes. They could use ICT.
> **For younger/less able younger children:** Let the children complete the photocopiable page without finishing the final part.

Missing person!

> **Objective:** To adapt non-narrative forms and styles to write fiction.
> **What you need:** Copies of *George's Marvellous Medicine*, paper, crayons or paints.
> **Cross-curricular links:** Citizenship; ICT.

What to do

● Discuss the ending of the story with the class and specifically how Mrs Kranky reacts when her mother disappears. Explain that you want them to imagine Mrs Kranky is unhappy about the disappearance and wants to find Grandma.

● Ask the children if they have ever seen any posters about missing people or animals, for example: lost cats. Encourage them to describe what sort of language and sentence structure these posters contain. (A heading, a question, a personal description, instructions, a photograph.)

● Hold a shared-writing session to create a poster advertising a lost dog or cat. Invite the children to suggest headings and write them on the board, for example: *LOST!* or *MISSING!* What information would be needed to give a clear description? (Size, shape, colour, sound, last seen.) Add suggestions to the board. What instructions would they need to give to anyone who finds the missing pet? Add these to the board. What other details of design and layout would help make the poster noticeable?

● Invite the children to create a Missing Person Poster about Grandma's disappearance.

● Make a wall display of the posters.

> **Differentiation**
> **For older/more able children:** Let the children use ICT to create their poster.
> **For younger/less able children:** Provide the children with sentence stems to help them, for example: *Grandma was last seen… She was wearing…* and so on.

Get writing

Headline news

Objective: To adapt non-narrative forms and styles to write fiction.
What you need: Copies of *George's Marvellous Medicine*, paper and pens.
Cross-curricular links: ICT.

What to do

● Ask the children to imagine a newspaper reporter has come to interview the family the day after Grandma disappeared. Say that Mr and Mrs Kranky wish to keep George's part in the disappearance a secret. Brainstorm ideas for a sensational headline, for example: *Vanishing Grandma in Disappearance Mystery*.
● Tell the children to work in groups of four to discuss questions a reporter might ask. Suggest that a reporter might be very curious about the odd-sized animals on the farm.
● Gather the children together and write their suggestions on the board. Create a list of words and phrases that are useful for writing journalistic text, including words to end quotations ('admitted', 'denied', 'added') and passive verb forms ('It has been reported…').
● Ask three children in the groups to play the characters in the story and the fourth child to act as the reporter. Encourage them to role play an interview, and then swap roles so that each has a turn to be the interviewer.
● Tell the children to write a news report about Grandma's disappearance, and invent some excuses or reasons why the events surrounding Grandma's disappearance cannot be explained.

Differentiation
For older/more confident learners: Ask the children to use ICT to create their reports using columns and paragraphs.
For younger/less confident learners: Work with the children to help them use formal language.

Change the ending

Objective: To experiment with different narrative forms and styles to write their own stories.
What you need: Copies of *George's Marvellous Medicine*, photocopiable page 29.
Cross-curricular links: ICT.

What to do

● Tell the class to re-read the last chapter of the book. Discuss the ending. Is it a satisfying ending? Did Grandma deserve to disappear? Has she really vanished or does she still exist somewhere?
● Encourage the children to think of other ways the story might have ended. Draw up a list of suggestions, for example: Grandma could have become tiny enough to live in a doll's house; the medicine might have changed her into a kindly old lady, or she might have grown even taller. Then, ask the children to suggest how George, and his parents would react to these new events. Would they change how they feel about Grandma?
● Let the children work with a partner and provide them with copies of photocopiable page 29. Tell them to record their ideas for an alternative ending. Once they have used the planning sheet in pairs, ask them to write their new endings individually.
● Discuss the children's ideas about the family's reactions and model how to make brief notes to the list of ideas for alternate endings. Explain that they are going to write their own alternate endings, first making brief notes of their ideas.
● Encourage the children to read their new story endings to their partner.

Differentiation
For older/more confident learners: Ask the children to use a computer to bring their writing to presentation standard.
For younger/less confident learners: Tell the children to write a new ending where Grandma turns into a kindly old lady. What might she say or do?

Get writing

Borrow the plot

> **Objective:** To experiment with different narrative forms.
> **What you need:** Copies of *George's Marvellous Medicine*, paper and pens.

What to do
● Discuss the plot of *George's Marvellous Medicine*. Ask the children to describe what happens as briefly as possible, and write a plot outline on the board, for example:

George has a mean Grandma. (Who)
He wants to teach her a lesson. (What)
George mixes up a new medicine. (How)
Grandma grows very big but she is pleased about this and still nasty.
George makes another medicine. Grandma drinks it though he warns her not to (Complication)
She shrinks and disappears. (Resolution)

● Explain that the children could reuse the plot to write their own story by changing some of the elements, for example, the characters: Grandma might be a mean big sister, or a visiting cousin. Ask the children to suggest other elements they could change, for example: a different way of teaching the character a lesson.
● Tell them to discuss, in pairs, how they could alter characters and events while using the plot, and to make a brief plan in note form.
● Ask some of the children to share their plans with the class. Could any improvements be made?
● Once the children are pleased with their story plans, ask them to choose three scenes from their own plan to write in detail.

> **Differentiation**
> For older/more **confident learners**: Encourage them to develop their stories over a longer period and write a full story in chapters.
> For younger/less **confident learners**: Ask them to write the story opening only.

Book review

> **Objective:** To appraise a text, deciding on its value and quality.
> **What you need:** Copies of *George's Marvellous Medicine*, photocopiable page 30.

What to do
● If possible, display some book reviews written by other children before beginning this activity. Talk about the purpose of a book review with the children. Ask them to suggest how a book review could influence their choices for reading.
● Discuss with the class their opinions about *George's Marvellous Medicine*. Did they enjoy it or not? Encourage them to support their opinions with examples from the story.
● Explain that they are going to write a book review about the story. Using the examples they have seen displayed, think of a list of the necessary features of book reviews, for example: title; author information; synopsis; most enjoyable and/or least enjoyable aspects of the story; the style of language; who would enjoy it; recommendation.
● Talk about the different sentence structures to use in a book review. For example, author information and synopsis needs impersonal sentences but favourite aspects are personal opinons and need personal language.
● Provide the children with copies of photocopiable page 30 and ask them to complete a book review for a class collection of reviews for *George's Marvellous Medicine*.

> **Differentiation**
> For older/more **confident learners**: Ask the children to write their book review without using the photocopiable sheet.
> For younger/less **confident learners**: Allow the children to omit the synopsis section.

Get writing

George's new sister

● Use the organiser to plan the character of George's new sister.

My name is

I am ____ years old.

What I like doing:
●
●
●

I think Grandma is…
●
●

What I don't like doing:
●
●
●

What I look like:
●
●
●

Things I like about George:
●
●

I say things like…
●
●
●

Things I dislike about George:
●
●

● Write a paragraph – What I think about George and his plan.

I think George is…

Change the ending

● Use the page to plan a new ending.

What happens to Grandma?

How does it happen?

What does Grandma say?

How does George react?

What does he say?

How does Mrs Kranky react?

What does she say?

How does Mr Kranky react?

What does he say?

Book review

Title	
Author	
About the author	
About the story	
The style of language (Write two examples of what you liked or disliked.)	
My favourite part	
My least favourite part	
Who would enjoy reading this book?	
Fill in the stars to grade the story.	☆ ☆ ☆ ☆ ☆

READ & RESPOND: Activities based on George's Marvellous Medicine

Assessment

Assessment advice

George's Marvellous Medicine follows the typical theme of many of Roald Dahl's stories, featuring an 'underdog' child as the hero who gets revenge on an unpleasant adult through a series of surreal events. It is unusual in that probably the most enjoyable part of the story consists of a chaotic process of mixing up ingredients as a recipe. This provides a good opportunity to assess children's ability to understand the importance of the order of events in a story and the idea of cause and effect. Ask them 'What happened when…?' questions as they read the story. Building on their understanding of sequential order, check that they remember the events of the story – what happened when George made his medicines two, three and four?

There are only four characters in the story,
so this provides good opportunities to assess children's awareness of how the author uses the characters' actions and dialogue to build details about them. Ask the children about how they think a character is feeling at certain points in the story, for example: George, just before he gives Grandma the new medicine; Grandma when her head pokes through the roof; Mr Kranky when he first sees the giant hen. Ask them for reasons to support their suggestions: what is there in the text that makes them think this? Does the character's dialogue or actions show readers what they are feeling?

Grandma's selfish personality is central to the plot. Ask the children to find examples, for instance: Why did Grandma drink Marvellous Medicine Number Four?

What happens next?

> **Assessment focus:** Understand how writers use different structures to create coherence and impact.
> **What you need:** Copies of *George's Marvellous Medicine*, photocopiable page 32, scissors, writing materials.

What to do
● Remind the children about the work they have done during reading on the sequence of events and cause and effect.
● Provide each individual child with a copy of photocopiable page 32. Without telling them that the list is taken from the chapter headings of *George's Marvellous Medicine*, ask the children to cut out the rows on the photocopiable sheet and place them in the correct order to show the
sequence of events in the story. Some children may recognise them as chapter headings; others may not recognise them when they are written using lower-case print.
● Once they have sequenced their cards, ask them to write a single sentence in the right-hand column for each of the headings. Explain that they can write whatever sentence they think is most relevant or important to illustrate how the key events progress through the story.
● Ask them to read each heading and their sentence one at a time and explain their choice of order and why they chose to write the sentence, that is: why they thought it most relevant or important.

What happens next?

the brown hen	
grandma	
George begins to make the medicine	
a crane for Grandma	
marvellous medicine number 2	
animal pills	
the marvellous plan	
Mr Kranky's great idea	
goodbye Grandma	
the pig, the bullocks, the two sheep, the pony and the nanny-goat	
the cook-up	
marvellous medicine number 4	
brown paint	
grandma gets the medicine	
marvellous Medicine number 3	